Like Water Running Off My Back

Like Water Running Off My Back

Poems by

Molefi K. Asante, Jr.

Africa World Press, Inc.

P.O. Box 1892   P.O. Box 48

Trenton, NJ 08607   Asmara, ERITREA

Africa World Press, Inc.

P.O. Box 1892
Trenton, NJ 08607

P.O. Box 48
Asmara, ERITREA

Book and Cover Design: Ashraful Haque

Catalog-in-Publication Data available from Library of Congress

ISBN 1-59221-006-6 (Hard cover)
ISBN 1-59221-007-4 (Paperback)

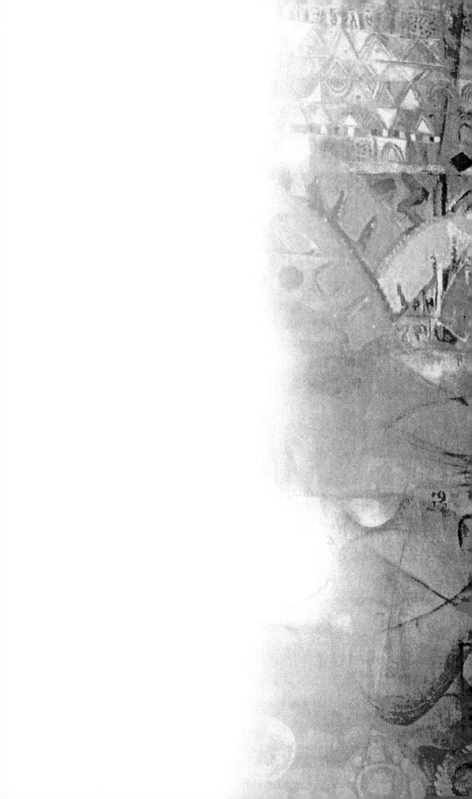

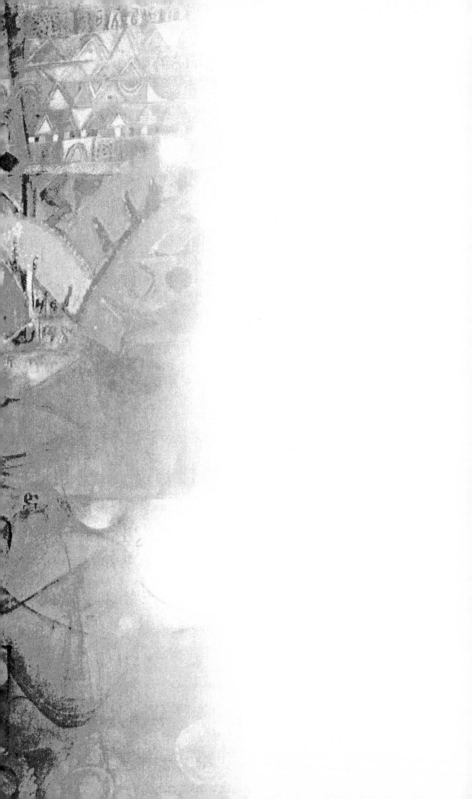

Contents

Acknowledgments

To my parents Molefi Kete and Kariamu Welsh Asante for the most precious gift-life; to my brother Daahoud, whose energy has inspired me; to my grandparents, Ruth Hoover, Arthur Smith, and Lillie Smith; to the original "teacha" Kevin Howie, for turning my eyes towards the truth and being a friend; to Deb Sotack and the Crefeld community for helping me express my ideas on paper; to Jon Sistrunk, Dustin Felder, and Anwar Lewis for being true friends; and finally, for all the poets who have inspired me, Amiri Baraka, Queen Goddess, Gil-Scott Heron, KRS-ONE, Talib Kweli, Ayi Kwei Armah, Dead Prez, Mos Def, Sonia Sanchez, Saul Williams, Kalamu ya Salaam, Allen Ginsberg, Jessica Moore, Ted Joans, Sherina Davis, Sarah Jones, Lee Upton, Post Midnight, Reiland Rabaka, Just Greg, Yolanda Wisher, Marvin Benjamin, Ross Gay, Robert Hayden, Brother D, Professor X, Chuck D, Aiesha Bradley, Misty, Kofi Opoku, Malik, Cazze, and Taj'el.
The Struggle Continues...

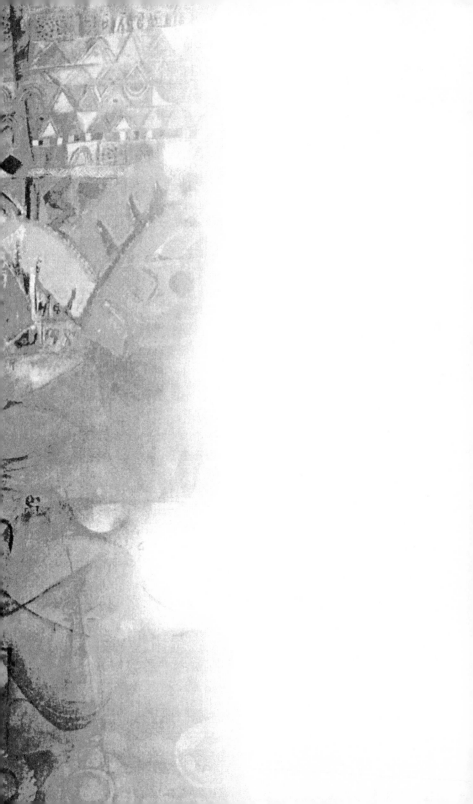

Libation

We call upon our ancestry
Who are scattered to the winds of the earth
Outstretched across oceans
Lying on continents both near and far
We call to the mothers who mothered our mothers
And to the fathers who fathered our fathers
We call upon the God (s) of the Earth in all guises
Asking to render mercy and to bare witness
For the liberation and victory of
oppressed peoples everywhere.

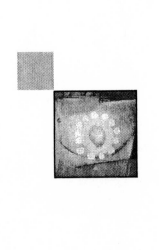

Absent Sun

As the sun approaches
movers of the mind
mingle through time
searching for street signs that bind my Inner Light
slowly seeping onto the papyrus of the night
igniting sight,
but I am only one,
dodging institutional dung
I dip and duck
to avoid being struck-
by lethal doses of hegemony-
that reverse roles and label me the enemy,
ain't that some shit
as if I came here on my own will-
on my own ship-without ownership,
I once bathed with Langston in the Euphrates
made love to the sun giving birth to seven brown babies
they sang the black blues
while I shined black and brown shoes-in back alleys
backed behind the windy echoes of Jim Crow Rally's
and Atlas,
the sun is approaching fast
and I stare hoping its rays will connect me with my past
removing the mask that covers my bronzed cast face

but never my mind

and a snail never leaves its shell behind

even in a foreign habitat,

so I don't adapt,

tuning God's tracks over 12inch wax

and the sun has approached us,

as it approaches, and is approaching

my mind is basking in the sun with souls soaking

in muddy waters with the sons and daughters of Nile

headwaters

who swim in purity

with high security from the sun

the same security that powers the sums of drums

which I now hum

because I used to live in fear,

why you ask,

because the sun wasn't here.

Time

If I could save time
I would stuff minutes under my mattress
and redefine backwards images of blackness
painted on prime time canvases by black actors and actresses
I would carry our history in my front pockets
and distribute it back without making a profit,
The result would be
a coming fourth by day
by night
sights still sitting steady
heavy as black burdens,
fist in air- Ready
To Die because living isn't living up to its half of the bargain
so we bargain and half-step with death-
ass betting our souls till nothings left
but the remnants of the oppressed
reeking of white sheets and the Negro that speaks of rivers
and I speak on lakes
stagnant,
reflecting our state
overflowing with collection plates filled to the top,
saddening me like the death of my grandpop,
or,
Hip-Hop...

REST IN PEACE
a sad day to say the least
and my radio's remarks are the marks of the beast
inviting me to feast,
but
I just ate,
and I'm not living to eat,
I'm living for the beat of drums
that talk through desolate slums
often the messages go unheard,
mis-communicated words
cause urban dreams to defer
and derail floating hopes,
as Ra sails across skies on solar boats
I can only hope
for brighter tomorrow's
because time can't be borrowed,
bottled, or bent
and if time was money
time could pay my rent
on time
but maybe I'm behind
because I'm on-
Colored Peoples Time
but I thought that today was
Colored Peoples Time
To shine like sunlight though African shrines

that are seemingly TIME—LESS

supposedly THIS

was BEFORE my time

but I'm trying to

Be-five

Be-six

Be-seven

Be-eight

Be-nine my time

And the truth is hard to find

in crime ridden cities that lead the blind

and produce wine from frozen vines

yet, the truth can be found

just as Nommo produces sound-waves

that behave in accordance with sun rays

dancing in imaginary rainbows

when the wind blows the rain

dropping the running man off

my windows stain glass pane

Two Thousand Seasons staying the same

as I walk in stride

alone

surrounded by nothing,

but Time.

Dear Rapper

To: The Highest Ranking Officer in the Black Community
From: The Black Community
Subject: Love

Dear Mr. Rapper,

I'm writing this letter because the love I once had for you has been lost, and I am hopeful that it can be regained. You don't know me personally, however you are the reason I am who I am today. As an adolescent, it was your influential lyrics that caused me to wear African medallions, believe that drugs and violence were forms of "Self Destruction", and even the reason why I write poetry today. Whether you're aware of it or not, being a Rapper perhaps plays the most essential role in shaping the minds and attitudes of black youths. As the most influential figure in the community, your popularity and influence supersedes that of our most prominent religious leaders, scholars, athletes, teachers, and even parents. Theoretically, if you decided tomorrow that you were going to wear dashikis and condemn violence, the result would be a generation of non-violent Afrocentrists. This is not to say that violence would be eradicated, or that wearing dashikis automatically makes you Afrocentric. However, it is to say that the attitudes of young people toward dashikis and violence would drastically change if you chose to change your rhymes. This is just one example of the power you possess.

In many ways, your influence resembles the influence the West African Djeli has on his village. Also known as a Griot by the French, Djelis are storytellers that teach moral, cultural, spiritual, and historical values through music and wordplay. In comparison, you possess the gift of storytelling and wordplay as a means of conveying ideas. Lately the ideas you've been conveying seem to only have a negative effect on our community. I've observed this negative affect first hand during my time tutoring inner city 2nd and 3rd graders. Even at such a young age, it's obvious rap has more influence on them then anything else, which is sad considering the current state of rap. From speech, to dress, to walk, almost all their actions are influenced by rap. However, those are just the visible aspects of rap's influence, the rabbit hole goes much deeper.

We live in an age where sadly, television and radio have a tremendous influence on our children, and in some cases literally raising them. The cyclical rotations of your songs that play on the radio subliminally teach a variety of ideological values to children. These values are then reinforced by your videos that play on music television channels like BET and MTV starting at around 3:00, when most children arrive home from school. Almost all of your videos depict lifestyles and philosophies that are detrimental to black youths. The emphasis on material possessions, the degradation of black women, and the glorification of criminal lifestyles are the central themes and messages in your songs, especially the ones that get heavy radio and video play. Often times the realities of the messages you convey are false even to you. Let's be realistic, You don't sell drugs! And there's a chance you never did, so why rap about it? And if you did sell drugs, you've seen the destruction it causes, so why glorify it then? We are all entitled to our own philosophies and the ways in which we view the world. However because of your position, your philosophies become the way our children view the world, and in turn, how the world views us.

I see the results of this saturation when I try to tutor my young students, instead of listening to their homework assignments, they'll recite lyrics about "fuckin bitches" and "rocking ice", Yes, 2nd graders. I know you're thinking, "I'm not solely to blame for the violence, materialism, and sexual exploitation of black kids". You're right, there are many other contributors that play a major role in destroying the minds of black youths. For example, radio stations, recording companies, and television channels all play major roles in this mental genocide. However, I've never had high moral expectations for large corporate entities that thrive on black exploitation. On the other hand, I've always had high expectations of my own brothers and sisters, but maybe I'm just naïve.
Sincerely,

The Black Community

Two Sets Of Notes for Black Students

I find myself feeling
as if I am touching the ground and the ceiling
in institutions that do not engage in healing
they simply open the wounds
and entrap me in rooms
where I am consumed by hypocrisy
but even Greek philosophers weren't the authors of their own
philosophy
And the statues on campus be watchin me'
Washington, Jefferson, William's
Clockin me'
as if to say 'my times up'
but I don't run laps on tracks
I run laps around the scholars of tomorrow
because their new schools of thought
are merely our histories borrowed
and they label me militant, and black national radical,
trying to put my learning process on sabbatical
I don't apologize
I spit truth into the whites of eyes infected by white lies
they even try to get me to See
there point of view from a brother that looks like ME
but that brother don't talk like me

walk like me
or act like me
and that brother turned his head
when I asked if he was black like me
mastering their thoughts
and forgetting your own
and you wonder why you always feel alone
from the Media to Academia
hanging brothers like coats
and in their schools
I always take two sets of notes
one set to ace the test
and one set I call the Truth
and when I find historical contradictions
I use the first set as proof
proof that black youths
Minds are being polluted,
convoluted, diluted,
Not culturally rooted
In anything
except the western massacre
and most of our children are scared of Africa
we view our mother's land
Through the eyes of Hume and Immauel Kant
Well
Immanuel can't tell me anything about a land he's never seen
a land rich with history

beautiful kings and queens

but they'll have you believe otherwise

their history is built on high rise lies

the pyramids were completed

before Greece or Rome were conceptualized

then they'll claim the Egyptians' race was a mystery

you tell them to read *Herodotus Book II* of the histories

can it be any clearer

Black children

look in the mirror

you are the reflection of divinity

don't let them fool you with selective memory

Walk High,

listen to the elders who spoke

Black Students,

ALWAYS TAKE TWO SETS OF NOTES!

Geometric Wars

There is death on both sides
but I can only see one side
however I am told there are many
in fact,
plenty
But my side died
many of them on their own side
while lying on their sides
and somehow I survived
managing to stay alive
on my own side
fighting against high tide,
for the eternal love of my side
Not for the love of a ride
for the love of my side I didn't hide
Instead I stood with pride,
eyes wide, arms at my side, ready to die for my side
inside and outside, what will spawn
I ask you,
What side are you on?

Like Water Running off My Back

Like water running off my back,
massaging my spine with gentle gestures transcribed in time
leaving space blindly behind
as I frantically search to find…Me
a reflection of divine ancestry,
who left shadows in the sunlight-
and pristine orange footprints in the shadows of the night,
listening to the esoteric echoes-
of Nommo when the wind blows-
through thick souls-corn rows-and afros
Two Thousand seasons ago
and Two Thousand seasons to go
blossoms, warmth, fallen rainbows, and snow
flooding my mental window…Until it is broken
The World is Sound!-
Poetry is to be spoken!
Either over influential instrumentals or silent beats,
because-remember, Silence is also speech!
So I speak in tongues infecting infantile eardrums
singing songs my grandmother sung-
dreaming about her grandfather who was hung,
not mistakenly, but blatantly
from an old Oak Tree-for the entire neighborhood to see

now witness me in my entirety

exuding of irony,

and ironically

I sit under an old oak tree

searching for traces of divinity-

or perhaps an infinite identity-

but that's both beyond my reality and my memory,

Forgetting the sinistry committed on this lands misery-

is the epitome of wickedrey-

it is not a mystery,

turn on your radio station

Without chains and whips,

poisoning our nations next generation,

claiming it doesn't have an affect

is like putting the noose around your own neck-

letting the DJ hang you,

while your children watch your feet dangle-

eagerly awaiting their turn to be strangled and mangled-

in the subconscious were they feed you garbage and nonsense-

in an attempt to make it sensible-

as if the children of the night were dispensable-

but we are not ,

somewhere along the way we must have forgotten the plot

AKA

The Master Plan

But I Got My Own Master Plan –

To Master The Plan - And Plan - The Masters Disaster!

and watch it collapse faster-
then the speed of light
penetrating the deeds of night which are jet black
And freedom is awaiting seven steps beneath that...
Like water,
running off ,my back.

Speech

Why do I speak?
A question that has plagued me for weeks
the answer comes in the form of cancerous stanzas,
seasons pass without speech-
yet I speak upon seasons,
those who don't understand
say I speak for no reason
but I breathe freely
knowing that the Ancestors can see me
and reflect like sunlight mirroring the black sea
I speak of Osirus Rising and Kenyatta listening to Mozart-
I speak of black soul,
black ice, and black art,
I am the voice of speechless souls-
and seamless scrolls-
embedded in the warmth of picked afros
I am,
the voice of metu neter-
giving life to dead lectures-
which becomes nectars for scholars in ghetto sectors
I see,
The children of the sun dancing in mobs-
in the reflection of the night reflecting gods,
we are

past visions of struggle that still ensue

Why do I speak?

I speak for you.

Urban Dreams

Sketches of shallow seas
with outstretched limbs shadowing me
and my existence
watching smoke tunnels twirling from lit incense
and I twirl through refined tunnels of time
looking for a way out
speaking in ways in which my reality can get out
running free like the burgundy energy streaming through, me-
Myself-and third I
reciting lullabies when tides are as high as skies seem
in urban dreams deferred
when herds of harsh words
are splurged on corners and curbs
where beautiful souls roam
far from home into tenement time zones
where Cops make frequent stops
Promoting Rock Minerals in the Subliminal
And Threaten to make our life sentences minimal
As If We Were The Actual Criminals,
so we take the fall
while they perpetuate oppressive criminal laws
look at their investment
don't be a freshman
they've tried to divide the skin

of the strongest women and men God will ever send

We are the children of tomorrow

sinking in the seas of yesterdays ideologies today

unaware of the omnipotent seventh sense

dense with matter,

but you tell me that ish don't matter

and how the stitching on western fabrics grow faster and

phatter

We are the messengers of life

dancing in the suns reflection of the night

You are the whistling windy echoes

giving birth to the revolutions manifestos

You are the medicine man,

Imhotep with pen in hand in the black soil of promised land

You are the children of tomorrow,

enacting futures unannounced,

moving truths by the ounce outweighing your past

but, time is moving fast,

and I can only imagine,

what is to become of a future that never happens

as if time was undisturbed

we must activate our words like verbs and leave time disturbed

WAKE UP

Lowly Life Drums

The drums of lowly life,
move into the darkness of lonely nights,
out of sight
too far to listen to echoes of men beating skin
heard in the wind by women time and again
until the sound penetrates minds
like Ogun penetrating shrines
as faces trapped in time
wait in imaginary lines
for reasons un-apparent
to the parents of the sun,
my seasons have sung to the rhythms of the drum
tracking sound
trapped and bound
in two different realities,
identical spirits separated
with distant mentalities
Our souls are the scrolls searching through streets
silently sitting at the same table with opposite seats
and we each sit on drums
humming neo Negro spirituals
and I've heard neo Griots perform nuance miracles
on dirt roads above project tenements
seemingly godsent

with branches sprightly bent over trees
and I've felt the Orixas speaking through me
at times
as if the thunder and the lightning weren't clear enough signs
in this lowly life insinuating me to come
And all I can hear is the echo from the Drum
silently vibrating the souls of lost slums
And all I can see is the echo from the Drum
vibrantly speaking to the children of the sun
And all I can be is the echo from the Drum.

The Door of No Return
(Goree Island)

I was told I couldn't return
yet, Sankofa tells me otherwise
so I stand surrounded by darkness,
slowly opening my eyes
Until the light blinds
like windows without blinds
shielding sunshine and unseen time
and time is just that,
unseen,
but I can see traces
And in bare blackness,
I can see familiar faces
faces that I have seen in dreams that seem real,
but beyond the sight of faces,
I can also feel
the outstretched limbs of my kin,
women and men with depleted dreams and shattered skin
taken from a foundation second to none,
Godnapping the original children of the sun
and I have returned
burned by truth,
navigated by dark faces that I am not supposed to see
yet they shadow me,

I can feel their pain as it still remains
combining with my own pain
our pains become the same
as are we,
you are the Ancestry the lives through me
shining like glimmering skies
You spit truth into my eyes!
I have accepted the gods,
and taken back your name,
calling to Iemanja when the skies cry with rain
Return home!
a message seemingly godsent,
given to me from a bird with its beak bent
standing in the doorway watching distant ships churn,
Nananom Nsamanfo (grandmother, grandfather)
I have returned.

Traces of a Generation for Allen Ginsberg

I

I didn't see the best minds of my generation,

out of sight,

viewless to the world,

consumed in an endless tunnel of time and space,

where their identities

were hidden behind commercial rap entities,

a Ritalin raised generation

drowning their livers in the nectars of the Gods

who hid behind the wild ecstasy of xanac driven tangents

That go on bawling about Annuit Coeptis and Illuminati

who sneak in the stillness of night,

depicting their world

through the movements of aerosol cans

a generation of corporate non-conformist,

refusing to wear ties that strangle necks and look silly.

II

A generation suffered,

forfeiting minds for machines,

ideas for idols,

innocence for ignorance.

who mis -

guided directions

and lost -

causes

causing them to simply exist

as an under the counter culture of poets

unswerving hysterically at the menopausal,

metallic, middle-aged minds

that have tried to corrupt their souls.

III

A generation of desolation...

Angels with out-stretched limbs,

holding on to false prophets-

who speak on city streets in the core of madness,

deceived souls,

polluted,

hiding behind satanic lyrics that hang over Littleton like fog,

who in isolation,

through cages, witness their brothers imprisoned in the black

shadows of white America,

who through madness,

become distorted and deaf to the once clamant and lucid

howling of their fathers,

who bear ambiguous relationships with America,

Us? Them? We?

who have moved so far left,

they are unswervingly right,

blinded behind alternative agendas.

IV

I witnessed my generation destroyed by Western madness,

still searching

in the machinery of night

for that ancient heavenly Kemetic connection to the stars,

still searching

for that last angry fix of truth

before

everything is revealed slowly across the torn canvas of life,

like traces of a generation generating light

Riddled Shots for Amadou Diallo

The number
Forty One rings in my mind
like death ringing when it's your time,
Not His
I'm convinced
stolen moments in past tense
And I'm Trying To Make It Make Sense!
but what good is sense
when brothers get lynched
by henchmen who never face suspension,
attempting to wipe out a race
with white out and black face
catching cases with stars and stripes in outer space
we reach for billfolds and get folded like dollar bills
writing wills before we're old enough to pay dollar bills
It saddens me,
to see another black casualty
of an invisible war
where's our War Mentality?
While white cops
continue to riddle black blocks
with white rocks and gunshots

don't depend on them to make it stop
their ice cold bitterness turns liquids into solids
and, and , I, was
Just reaching,
For my wallet…

Horny (Jazz)

I can hear melodies

ringing in my head like cerebral secular cellulars,

echoes of Armstrong

play in my thoughts strong like long nights

Dreaming of black horns,

the soundtrack of my life

filled with tissue thin notes

floating like lost spirits

can you hear it?

Communicating without lyrics

like talking drums

the horns scream through slums

bawling notes with chords-cherry sweet

forever lulling my jazzy soul to sleep

Rebuilding A Nation

How can I suffer from writers block
when writers on God's block suffer from shots and dodge cops
I sit studying Ma'at
searching for possible answers
singing divine words with angels as back up dancers
Dancing for freedom
the antecedent of death
doing my best
with Horus, to defeat Set
Digging in crates
for our past stored in memory banks
but they've even robbed
Our Memories Banks
allowing our heroes to be deposited as urban legends
as we invest checks to buy cars for the reverend
we are far from home
when I compete with cell phones
to radiate my peoples domes
but, I must be heard
so I speak
with four hundred years of words
built on Kemetic limestone's,
one by one
We are the children of The Stars,
The Moon, and The Sun

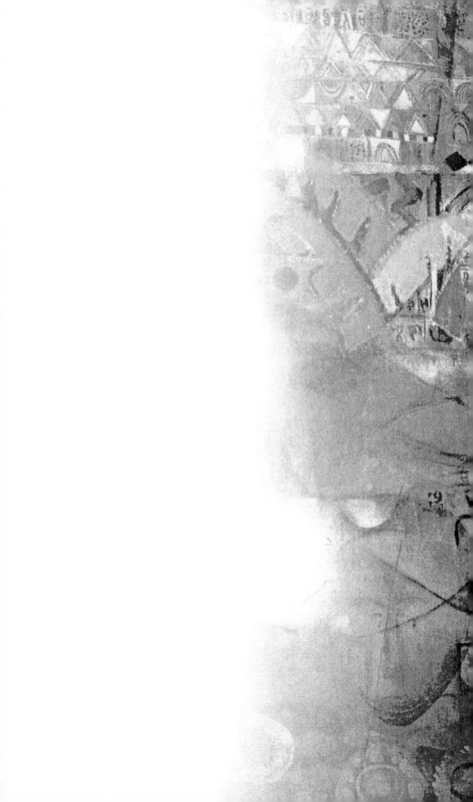

Umfundalai Verse

Umfundalai is an African American verse form created by poet, Kariamu W. Asante. Umfundalai is derived from a five-seven symbolic, syllabic and rhythmic structure based on the poly-rhythms of Africa. The form strives to utilize Afrocentric symbols in a manner that dictates economy of words and an authoritative ending. Like the European sonnet, the Japanese haiku, the African American umfundalai represents discipline, art, and the people's voice. Unlike the haiku and sonnet, umfundalai is rooted in African American history.

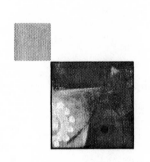

Amerikas "New" War

In the civil war
we were not treated as men,
Yankees in battle
just to be niggas again
so we sang the blues
while we died for you without
shoes, to keep our feet
from the ice blistering cold
fifty years before,
mothers and fathers were sold

We lost too many
too many lost for God's sake
it will not happen again
that battle, was a mistake

This time was the French
but here, our brothers were lynched
hanging from trees like
swinging vines and autumn leaves,
over seas we shipped out
fingers on rusty triggers
Woodrow calls France, to
ensure treatment as Niggers

we lost too many
too many lost for Gods sake
it will not happen again
that battle was a mistake

Twenty years later
blacks are needed to war more

It's not the first, but
It is the Second World War
days under attack
left out to dry "there just blacks",
defeated Hitler
and stopped the white iron sword
when we returned home
of course, no awards,
some black men fought to the end
sailed across the sea
and were not docked in
they starved on U.S waters,
is this the story
you tell your sons and daughters?

we lost too many
too manylost for Gods sake
it will nothappen again
that battle was amistake

After travesty
Please! No more black casualties
five years after that
and the same mentality,
no hesitation
to go fight in Korea
now we hesitate
to go fight for Mumia,
we fought separate
from whites in different divisions
but, on death missions
and we managed to survive
and to stay alive
for three very grueling years
among tattered tears,
shattered fears, and battered peers

welost too many
toomanylost for Gods sake
it will not happenagain
that battle was amistake

and eight years later
black and still bloody from bombs
you asked us to go
fight your war in Vietnam,
many of us blacks
didn't know what that war meant
but enough questions
and with that, we quickly went
off to fight again
for a decade and a half
many were wounded
and some couldn't stand to last
we were the point men
which meant we led the whole plot
but realistically,
it meant the first to be shot
came home missing limbs
but had a plaque for our dens,
came back not the same
insane scenes, infected brains

welosttoomany
toomanylostforGodssake
itwillnothappenagain
thatbattlewasamistake

and five years later
even more war for us blacks
dropped bombs on the ghetto
and they exploded with crack-
cocaine for black brains
to ease black pains

dealers got gold platinum chains,
can't you see brother
the war is happening here
in front of your face,
no need to go over there!

Twenty years later
Thinking of American's sin
Asking me to fight!
But, it won't happen again

Molefi K. Asante Jr

Black Words for Amiri Baraka

Nothing More to Say
inspiring me to write
You should have seen me
reading *Black Art* at midnight
igniting fires
with loud flames changing my frame,
my thoughts weren't the same!
Dreams of poetic screams that stream
through minds of black teens

You paint the pictures
on pages- for brothers in and
outside of cages
with an hour of sunshine
You illuminate
light through black lifetimes because-
you are the lifeline
for generations deferred
revolutions' words
and our actions are your verbs

You activate souls
for *Blues People* with afros
and men of the sun,

from lands where ancestors hung
your voice is the drum
Beating a Generation
of poets from slums
The night in autumn is red
Poetry...not dead
Living like Sankofa Birds
Singing, your Black Words

Sankofa Still Waiting

Smelling wounds of war,
which, for us, is metaphor
like a rose in stone
and right above my window-
sankofa has flown
but, the fool travels alone,
so if my people-
can't return home, I sit in
darkness writing poems

Blanket of Love

At our weakest points
I am the strength you anoint
solid and steady
tending to tattered tears heavy
with wounds from above
dressing your wounds with my blood
undying as love
through great lengths, you and I are
each others source of strength

The Peoples Shadow

The peoples shadow
moving where the people move
shadowing our steps
you reflect us in mirrors
in speech and in life
through the trials of day and night
The Peoples Shadow

Nkonsonkonson For Malauna Karenga

The Chain that links US
far from chains that brought US here
but the chains have changed
shining hope on lights' sphere
with flaming candles
lit by the ancestors drum
Nkonsonkonson

Unmasking Love

Sometimes love's unseen
like vacant battered eyes torn,
but it's always there
because when you leave, I mourn
crying tears of rain
stained by your hidden love, like
hands, hiding in gloves

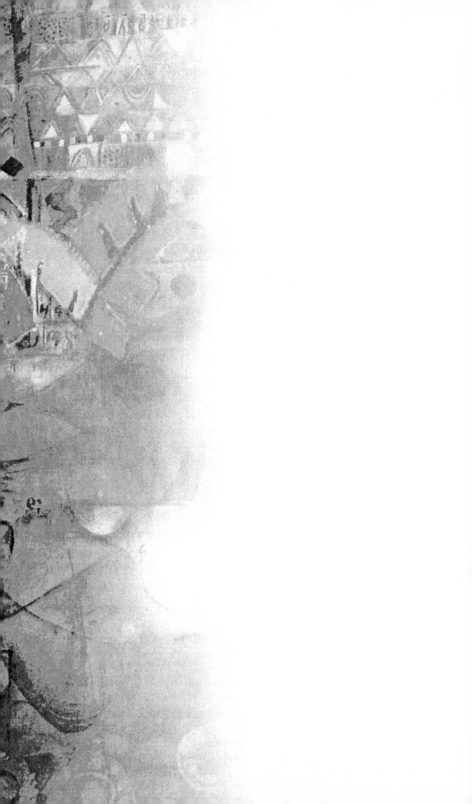

Glossary of Selected Terminology

Annuit Coeptis- A Latin term meaning A New Concept

Euphrates- A river in Asia

Goree Island- Located off the coast of Senegal, a slave fortress where enslaved Africans were kept before being shipped to the Americas

Griot- West African keeper of traditions through music and storytelling

Imhotep- Ancient Egyptian architect who design step pyramid, also a mathematician and scientist

Kenyatta Listening to Mozart- A Poem by Amiri Baraka

Ma'at- Ancient Kemetic idea of justice, harmony, balance, order, righteousness, truth, and reciprocity

Metu Neter- Ancient Egyptian term meaning sacred words, also known as hieroglyphics by the Greeks

Nananom- Grandmother in the Twi language

Nile- A river in Egypt, Africa

Nkonsonkonson- Twi word, meaning the chain that links us together

Nommo- The utterance power of the word

Nsamanfo- Grandfather in the Twi language

Ogun- The orishas of iron and war

Orisha- Yoruba spirits that control the elements

Osirus Rising- A historical novel by Ayi Kwei Armah

Ra- Egyptian god of the sun

Sankofa- Represented by a bird with its beak turned 180 degrees, literally means return home

Two Thousand Seasons- A historical novel by Ayi Kwei Armah